The Declaration DECODED

A GUIDE TO THE DOCUMENT THAT INSPIRED OUR NATION

KATIE KENNEDY

Workman Kids
New York

For Patrick—

I would take on an empire with you by my side

Workman Kids
Workman Publishing
Hachette Book Group, Inc.
1290 Avenue of the Americas
New York, NY 10104
workman.com

Workman Kids is an imprint of Workman Publishing, a division of Hachette Book Group, Inc. The Workman name and logo are registered trademarks of Hachette Book Group, Inc.

Design by Daniella Graner

Library of Congress Cataloging-in-Publication Data is on file.

ISBN 978-1-5235-3520-0

Ebook ISBN 978-1-5235-3522-4

First Edition April 2026

Printed in Dongguan, China (01/26) TEX on responsibly sourced paper

10 9 8 7 6 5 4 3 2 1

CONTENTS

NOT DOMINION, BUT LIBERTY

The Declaration of Independence is the United States' first and most important document of resistance. It rejected tyranny and declared Americans to be a free people, able to govern themselves and bowing to no king. In July 1776, the Second Continental Congress adopted the Declaration, announcing the birth of a new nation. It rocked the world.

The Declaration proclaimed new principles: equality, liberty, self-determination, the right to overthrow bad governments, the concept that power resides with the people. It is a triumph of optimism, the belief that change is possible, that government exists to improve the lives of its citizens. With its signing, America "spoke herself into existence," as John Quincy Adams said, adding that its "glory is not dominion, but liberty. Her march is the march of the mind." America wasn't just a new nation: It was a new idea.

On July 10, 1858, in the midst of his campaign for an Illinois Senate seat, Abraham Lincoln noted that high rates of immigration meant "perhaps half our people . . . are not descendants at all of [the Signers] . . . but when they look through that old Declaration of Independence they find that those old men say that 'We hold these truths to be self-evident, that all men are created equal,' and then they feel . . . that they have a right to claim it as though they were blood of the blood, and flesh of the flesh, of the men who wrote that Declaration, and so they are." He continued, "That is the electric cord in that declaration that links the hearts of patriotic and liberty-loving men together, that will link those patriotic hearts as long as the love of freedom exists in the minds of men throughout the world."

The Declaration has been the electric cord binding our hearts ever since it was signed, in that hushed, hallowed moment when courage met danger. The text is, in the words of historian Pauline Maier, "American scripture." It is inscribed on our hearts.

When the fifty-six delegates from thirteen colonies signed the document, they were reacting to a long series of British political decisions, ranging from the irritating to the infuriating. These decisions grew out of Britain's triumph over France in the French and Indian War, which lasted from 1754 until 1763. The victory resulted in the British controlling a great deal more North American territory—including the 200,000-square-mile Ohio River Valley—which would cost much more to run. Add in a staggering war debt, and the British

Parliament needed to raise money to support these suddenly very expensive colonies. With the war, Britain also began to pay more attention to American affairs, ending its previous policy of "salutary neglect" (leaving the colonies alone, which benefited them).

In an effort to deal with these postwar issues, Britain issued the Proclamation of 1763, which halted westward migration at the crest of the Appalachian Mountains. The measure helped Indigenous people and Britain's new French-Canadian colonists. But to English colonists on the seaboard, hoping to make fortunes in the West, Britain had given away their future—to the people they'd just fought and defeated. It made no sense to them, and it came as the colonial economy sank into a depression.

Over the next few years, Parliament imposed more restrictions on colonial trade. In 1764, it passed the Sugar Act, taxing colonial exports, and the Currency Act, preventing colonists from printing their own paper money. The next year it instituted the Quartering Act, which required American civilians to house British troops at their own expense.

The Stamp Act of 1765, which taxed printed material, prompted furious colonists to send delegates to a national assembly. This "Stamp Act Congress" was only the second time representatives from most colonies had gathered together, and it rejected Parliament's right to tax colonists when they had no representation in that body. William Pitt the Elder, the British statesman whose policies had won the French and Indian War—and created the national debt that now needed to be paid off—agreed with the colonists. "I would fain to know by whom an American is represented here," he thundered in Parliament. Colonial opposition got the Stamp Act repealed, and the colonies discovered they could work together to defend their interests.

Britain continued to pass acts designed to raise revenue, which colonists resisted by refusing to buy British goods. In 1767 the Townshend Acts taxed glass, lead, paint, paper, and tea, which should have increased British revenue. Some of that money was used to pay the salaries of colonial judges, making them dependent on Britain. Colonists thought the Townshend Acts reduced their liberty. Then Parliament made it worse by sending troops to America, which led to conflict with local citizens. The most serious incident was the 1770 Boston Massacre, in which British troops opened fire on a crowd that had been harassing them, killing several civilians.

In response to a colonial boycott of British goods, Parliament ended the tax on glass, paper, and paint, but not tea. Then in 1773, it gave the British East India Company a monopoly on tea imports. That wasn't meant to rile up the colonists, but it did. They objected to any tax, even a low one, when they didn't have representation in Parliament. The issue wasn't just economics; it was justice. When three ships carrying the tea arrived in Boston, colonists dumped their cargoes into the harbor. That resulted in harsh reprisals from London. The five laws known in Britain as the Coercive Acts—and as the Intolerable Acts in the colonies—passed in 1774 in response to the Boston Tea Party, removed a number of the colonists' rights and closed the port of Boston. It was a huge economic blow.

The colonists again gathered in response, sending delegates to the First Continental Congress, which met for seven weeks in late 1774. The Congress didn't do much, but it helped create a new sense of common identity. Patrick Henry said, "The distinctions between Virginians, Pennsylvanians, New Yorkers, and New Englanders, are no more. I am not a Virginian, but an American." The Congress agreed to meet again in six months if things hadn't settled down.

By the time the Second Continental Congress came together in May 1775, fighting had already started. The previous month, British troops tried to seize arms in Concord, Massachusetts—and possibly seize rebel leaders, too. They marched through Lexington on the way; shots were fired there, and colonists won a battle in Concord. The Battle of Bunker Hill followed in June, also in the Boston area. With British troops and colonists facing each other in open battle, it was impossible to go back. There would be war.

The colonists made one last-ditch effort to reconcile. In July 1775, Congress sent the Olive Branch Petition to King George III, who refused to read it. John Dickinson, Congress's leading peace advocate, had drafted the petition. It had no chance, but after letting Dickinson take his shot, it was easier to move forward and face the

★ TRANSPORTATION ★

By today's standards, there was a mind-blowing delay between events occurring on one side of the Atlantic and news of them arriving on the other side. Without the Internet, satellites, phones, or even telegraphs, both colonists and the British communicated via written documents sent across the ocean on sailing ships. How long did a ship take to cross the Atlantic? About four or five weeks, but that time varied enormously depending on the type and size of vessel, how much cargo it carried, and what time of year it made the voyage. The experience level of the captain and crew mattered, too, and so did random accidents. The biggest variable was the weather. In the age of sail, wind was critical, but ice,

reality that thirteen colonies were about to confront an empire. This Second Continental Congress raised an army and put George Washington in command. And this was the body that in July 1776 would vote for independence, drafting a declaration to explain itself.

It was a remarkable step. Americans would now elect delegates to represent their interests, rejecting centuries of monarchy, in which the right to rule was passed

fog, air pressure, and sea surface temperature all made a difference, too.

Transportation within British America was difficult as well. The colonies didn't have major highways, so most travel between colonies was done by ships that hugged the coast to go up or down the seaboard or sailed on rivers into a colony's interior. What roads existed were often in poor repair and sometimes impassable due to weather. The trip from Boston to Philadelphia, for example, which today takes about five and a half hours by car, took about two weeks and required six ferry crossings.

The result of slow travel, of course, was a weeks-long delay in transatlantic communication. And mail could and did get lost—including one of the first copies of the Declaration itself.

down within a family. By declaring their independence, Americans seized their freedom and the right to rule themselves. They announced that in the United States, a government's legitimacy came not from bloodlines but from the ballot. In the United States, people were equal. They had rights that could not be taken away. And they would stand against the mightiest empire in the world—and not blink.

It would take the victories of the Continental Army to secure independence, and the writing of the US Constitution to turn the Declaration's ideals into law. Those aspirations were not fully realized; the US was, after all, a nation in which slavery was legal, and only white men could vote. But the Declaration laid down an enduring framework of American political ideals—the ones we still strive for today.

INDEPENDENCE LIKE A TORRENT

January 1776 was a pivotal month for the American colonies. They finally heard the news that in late October 1775, King George III had given a speech to Parliament in which he had said he would send mercenaries (soldiers hired from other countries) to North America. The speech met with approval in both houses of Parliament, which then passed the Prohibitory Act, ending the colonies' trade with other nations and letting the Royal Navy seize American ships. It also ended the king's protection over the colonies: Colonists were now to be treated as enemies. Word also came that a fleet carrying five thousand troops had set sail for America and that British troops had burned Norfolk, Virginia, on the first day of the year. These events stunned—and infuriated—colonists.

In the second week of January, in the midst of this brutal run of news, Thomas Paine's pamphlet *Common Sense* was published. Paine used everyday language to point out problems with the British government. It wasn't just that the king had a few bad advisors, he said; hereditary monarchy *itself* had to go. This was a world-upending proposal. In 1776, the Netherlands and Switzerland were both governed as republics, but neither was what Paine envisioned: a unified nation where all power came from popular choice and none was reserved for hereditary rulers (like a queen or king, or the nobility). "We have it in our power," he wrote,

★ BRITISH RIGHTS AND COLONIAL REPRESENTATION ★

In 1688, William and Mary ousted King James II of England in a coup known as the Glorious Revolution. The revolutionary settlement the following year included passage of a Bill of Rights. It proclaimed that Parliament, and the people who elected its members, had rights the monarchs could not overrule. They could not collect taxes or engage in a foreign war without Parliament's consent. They could not maintain a standing army in peacetime. And the Crown could not interfere with elections or dismiss the legislature. Parliament asserted itself as an equal branch of government with the king and queen.

Colonists considered their own legislatures to have the same rights as Parliament. They felt that

"to begin the world over again." *Common Sense* sold for eighteen pence, which most people could afford, and perhaps 150,000 copies circulated in the colonies alone. It got people talking about what gives a government the right to rule. When Congress declared independence six months later, it reflected the national mood. Much of that was because of Thomas Paine.

their assemblies, too, should be free of interference by the Crown. After all, as British citizens, they were protected by the 1689 Bill of Rights, which had been explicit about not taxing people without their consent through their representatives. When Britain began to pay more attention to the colonies after the years of "salutary neglect," Parliament interfered in ways that colonists thought weren't allowed. Did they not have the same rights as any other Englishmen?

To the authorities in Britain, the answer was "no." They claimed colonists didn't need actual representation in Parliament because they had "virtual representation"—that English legislators considered everyone's needs when passing laws, and so colonists didn't need to make their voices heard.

The colonists did not agree.

There was danger in declaring independence—but there was also danger in having no government, and the colonial governments that English rulers had put in place decades before no longer functioned. Individual colonies had begun asking the Second Continental Congress for authority to set a government up; they needed some sort of order. Colonies also had overlapping land claims in the west. At some point, they would have to deal with those claims, and settling the issue would require a level of government higher than the colonies themselves. If there would be no more king, the colonies needed to band together in a confederation. Action could be deadly, but so could inaction.

In May 1776, Congress passed a resolution telling the colonies to set up the governments that seemed best to them. A committee was charged with writing a preface for the resolution; a cantankerous Massachusetts lawyer named John Adams did the writing. He presented it to the Congress three days later—and it was radical. (That was no surprise; no delegate was more pro-independence than Adams.) The preamble listed grievances against Britain and then said, ". . . it is necessary that the exercise of every kind of authority under the said crown should be totally suppressed, and all the powers of government exerted, under the authority of the people of the colonies . . ." All power to the people of the colonies? That's independence. John Adams wrote to his wife, Abigail Adams, that the resolution, passed with its preface on May 15, was "a total, absolute Independence," but that a declaration to the effect would still be necessary.

Colonies and towns began drafting their own resolutions advocating independence from Britain, which they forwarded to the Congress. By the time Congress passed its own Declaration in July, some ninety other declarations had been approved—by nine colonies, more than fifty towns, and even a Pennsylvania militia battalion and a group of New York mechanics. In late May, John Adams said that with the arrival of each day's mail, independence "rolls in upon Us . . . like a torrent."

The most important resolution came from Virginia, as its convention called for both independence and a union of the colonies. On Friday, June 7, Virginia delegate Richard Henry Lee presented its resolution to Congress. John Adams seconded the resolution, which read in part that "*these United Colonies are, and of right ought to be, free and independent States*," language that would be included in the final Declaration.

Congress debated Lee's resolution for two days, then tabled it for three weeks. This delay was intentional. If the resolution came to a vote, delegates would be voting explicitly for independence, and not all the colonies had given their delegates the power to make that vote. Some delegations needed time to receive new orders.

In the meantime, it would be handy to have an announcement of the country's independence ready, because timing could become important. Until the colonies were independent, European nations couldn't negotiate with them, or even let American ships in their harbors. The colonies would need French aid to defeat Britain, but if they declared independence and France didn't send help, they were no worse off than before. But if the colonies didn't declare, Britain might make its own alliance with France, agreeing to split North America. France could take back the territory it lost in the French and Indian War, and with France neutralized, Britain would surely regain control over its wayward colonies. The colonists needed to declare their freedom before Britain started whispering in France's ear.

On June 11, Congress appointed a Committee of Five to draft its own declaration of independence, which would explain the reasons for the colonies' separation from Britain. The committee consisted of John Adams of Massachusetts, Benjamin Franklin of Pennsylvania, Roger Sherman of Connecticut, Robert Livingston of New York, and from Virginia, Thomas Jefferson, who had only recently arrived in Philadelphia. Members of the committee were also given other committee assignments while working on the Declaration. In a six-month period in 1775 and 1776, Jefferson served on approximately thirty-four congressional committees.

According to Adams, writing decades later, the Committee of Five had "several meetings, in which were proposed the Articles of which the Declaration was to consist, and minutes made of them." They created an outline, in other words, and written instructions for what to include in a first draft. Adams said the committee then chose him and Thomas Jefferson to do the actual writing, and Jefferson urged Adams to take the outline and notes and write the draft. Adams declined on the basis that "1. That he was a Virginian and I a Massachusettensian. 2. That he was a southern Man and I a northern one. 3. That I had been so obnoxious for my early and constant Zeal in promoting the Measure, that any draught of mine, would undergo a more severe Scrutiny and Criticism in Congress, than one of his composition. 4thly and lastly that would be reason enough if there were no other, I had a great Opinion of the Elegance of his pen and none at all of my own . . ." So Jefferson wrote the draft. Adams was right on all fronts: Much of the early resistance to Britain had taken place in New England, and Congress wanted to make it clear that independence wasn't a regional issue; Jefferson wrote beautifully; and Adams could be extremely annoying.

When Adams's version of events came to Jefferson's attention years later, he grumbled that Adams was mistaken and said the Committee had asked only *him* to write the draft. That was probably true. Adams's memory seems to have increased his role, especially since he recorded in his diary in June 1779—only three years later—that *Jefferson* had been appointed to write the Declaration. If Adams had also been asked, he surely would have mentioned it. Either way, it was Jefferson who wrote the draft. Since Jefferson enslaved people, unlike Adams, that decision attached lasting irony to a document declaring all men to be created equal.

That said, Jefferson was the logical choice because of his writing skill and general knowledge. A genius who knew at least six languages, conducted scientific experiments, and was a talented innovator, he understood the new science of the Scientific Revolution, and he had read widely in Enlightenment thought, with its emphasis on liberty, reason, and religious skepticism and toleration. In particular, he had read the works of English philosopher John Locke, and echoes of Locke's ideas from *Second Treatise of Civil Government* can be found in the Declaration, including the idea that governments exist to protect the rights of the governed.

Jefferson drew on other texts as well. He had just written the preamble for the Virginia constitution, in which he made charges against the king. He listed those charges again in the Declaration and added some new ones. He had also read George Mason's early version of the Virginia Declaration of Rights, and he had both it and his Virginia preamble on hand in Philadelphia. In the eighteenth century, there was no shame attached to borrowing from other documents in a piece of writing—especially if you did a good job. In 1823 Jefferson wrote to James Madison that he "did not consider it part of my charge to invent new ideas altogether, and to offer no sentiment which had ever been expressed before."

Who was the Declaration written for? It had three audiences. One was the British, as a break-up letter. The second was the world at large, to announce the birth of the United States. One country among the world's nations was the most important, however, and that was France; French military support would be crucial in the coming fight, and everyone knew it. It would be easier to get aid once the US was a nation, but a document denying the rights of kings and insisting that governments get their powers from the consent of their people? That wasn't written to win over King Louis XVI. The most crucial of the three audiences, then, was the colonists themselves. The Declaration was meant to build morale and give the colonists a clear reason for fighting. They were about to take on their mother country, which had solidly beaten France in the last war. It was a daunting prospect. Jefferson's words steadied their hearts and strengthened their hands.

What he created was an astonishing document—a passionate defense of the rights of people against kings.

THE UNANIMOUS DECLARATION

THE PREAMBLE

The Declaration is structured in three parts. The Preamble, or introduction, sets up the right of revolution; the Grievances make the case for it in the colonies; and then the Formal Declaration of Independence invokes that right. The Preamble is inspirational and aspirational. It contains some of the most beautiful phrases of any American document and lays foundational ideals for Americans of that time, and of ours.

In Congress, July 4, 1776
The unanimous Declaration
of the thirteen united States of America

When in the Course of human events, it becomes necessary for one people to dissolve the political bands which have connected them with another, and to assume among the powers of the earth, the separate and equal station to which the Laws of Nature and of Nature's God entitle them, a decent respect to the opinions of mankind requires that they should declare the causes which impel them to the separation.

DECODED **The joint declaration of the thirteen United States of America:**

When one group of people must split off from their previous country to create a new nation—which natural law gives them the right to do—they should explain why they're separating.

The Declaration didn't create American independence. The adoption of Richard Henry Lee's resolutions by the Congress did that (bolstered, of course, by the ultimate victories of the Continental Army). Instead, it was a trumpet blast to the world and to the residents of the colonies proclaiming that a new nation had arisen. Since the Declaration would be read out loud to jostling crowds, it needed to pack a punch from the beginning. This first sentence is remarkably long—seventy-one words—but it conveys a sense of drama and urgency. It also announces a reason for the Declaration's existence: to "declare the causes" behind the separation from Britain.

In the first masterful stroke of many, Jefferson writes of "one people," rather than "these colonies," immediately setting a tone of unity among all Americans. This is not another petition to the king asking him to address their problems; it is a powerful statement from a people rising to claim their rights and join the ranks of nations. "Mankind" here refers to other countries, who are being informed of a new peer standing among them.

Jefferson's primary idea here is the right of revolution—he presents it before saying an explanation is required, which presumably was the point of the paragraph. "Dissolve" is the fifteenth word, because Jefferson doesn't hide his point: Natural law gives people the right to free themselves from bad government—to revolt.

When Jefferson refers to natural law, he means the fundamental principles of the universe itself, as natural laws have an authority deeper and more profound than the laws of a king. Talk of natural law came from the Enlightenment, an intellectual movement based on the principles of the Scientific Revolution and a belief in progress and reason. Astronomers had proven that there was order to the universe. Eclipses, for example, were predictable phenomena, not signs of divine anger.

Jefferson was a Deist—someone who believes that God created the laws of nature but that He didn't get involved in human affairs. Deists picture God as a watchmaker who wound a clock and then let it run by itself. Jefferson had an Enlightenment skepticism of organized religion, and while God (as "Providence") is mentioned again later in the document, that addition wasn't Jefferson's.

The Declaration of Independence became unanimous when the New York delegation received new instructions from its colonial legislature on July 15 and its delegates were finally able to vote for the document.

We hold these truths to be self-evident, that all men are created equal, that they are endowed by their Creator with certain unalienable Rights, that among these are Life, Liberty and the pursuit of Happiness.—That to secure these rights, Governments are instituted among Men, deriving their just powers from the consent of the governed, —That whenever any Form of Government becomes destructive of these ends, it is the Right of the People to alter or to abolish it, and to institute new Government, laying its foundation on such principles and organizing its powers in such form, as to them shall seem most likely to effect their Safety and Happiness.

DECODED It's clear to all of us that all people are equal and that they have certain God-given rights that can't be taken away, including life, liberty, and the pursuit of happiness. Governments are created to protect these rights and are only legitimate if the people agree to give the government power. If a government stops protecting people's rights, the people who live under it have the right to change or overthrow it. Then they can create a new government of whatever type they think will best make them safe and happy.

"We hold these truths to be self-evident . . ." is one of the most famous lines ever written by an American. It's a rare bit of writing that encapsulates an entire world in one sentence, like a political snow globe. This passage contains the heart of what it means to be an American: People have rights, the government can't take them away, and the government only exists to secure those rights. The pursuit of property was an idea a number of European and colonial writers had discussed; that Jefferson here changed it to the pursuit of "happiness" is striking. He may have been concerned that "pursuit of property" sounded like support for slavery. Although himself an enslaver, Jefferson chipped away at slavery on multiple occasions—including later in the Declaration itself.

This passage also attacks hereditary monarchy, in which one family passed down the right to rule through their children. Monarchies are not legitimate, Jefferson says, because they deny the people's right to self-government. Thomas Paine had made the same point in *Common Sense* when he wrote that "all men being originally equals, no *one* by *birth* could have a right to set up his own family in perpetual preference to all others for ever." The Declaration says it better: "all men are created equal"—a bedrock American political principle.

That the truths were "self-evident" may have been Franklin's addition; Jefferson had originally written "sacred & undeniable." When Congress revised the Committee of Five's draft, it didn't change much in the early paragraphs; an exception is "inherent and inalienable rights," which became "certain inalienable rights." "Inalienable" seems to have become "unalienable" through a printing error.

Prudence, indeed, will dictate that Governments long established should not be changed for light and transient causes; and accordingly all experience hath shewn, that mankind are more disposed to suffer, while evils are sufferable, than to right themselves by abolishing the forms to which they are accustomed. But when a long train of abuses and usurpations, pursuing invariably the same Object evinces a design to reduce them under absolute Despotism, it is their right, it is their duty, to throw off such Government, and to provide new Guards for their future security.

DECODED Common sense indicates that governments that have been around for a long time shouldn't be changed for petty reasons. Experience shows that people are more likely to put up with bad government than get rid of one they're used to. But when a clear pattern emerges of a government abusing people and stepping on their liberties, it is the people's right and duty to leave that government and put in protections so they'll be safer in the future.

John Locke had written in his *Second Treatise of Civil Government* that people should "rouze themselves" against the government only after a "long train of Abuses, Prevarications, and Artifices . . ." Jefferson echoes the "long train of abuses" here—just one place where Locke's influence is apparent. In an early draft, Jefferson had said that such a train of abuses led to "arbitrary power," and Franklin, or possibly Adams and Franklin, edited it to read "absolute Despotism." Most edits toned down the fire in Jefferson's draft, but this one ramped it up.

—Such has been the patient sufferance of these Colonies; and such is now the necessity which constrains them to alter their former Systems of Government. The history of the present King of Great Britain is a history of repeated injuries and usurpations, all having in direct object the establishment of an absolute Tyranny over these States. To prove this, let Facts be submitted to a candid world.

DECODED These colonies have been putting up with a bad government that abuses their rights; and now they need to change their government. The present king of Great Britain has repeatedly infringed on the people's rights, trying to create an oppressive rule over these States. We will prove it to the world.

It was British tradition to blame the king, not Parliament, when announcing that a government had lost its legitimacy, but the references to "repeated injuries" and "absolute Tyranny" make this more personal than the usual attacks. Jefferson is stoking the fire here because next he jumps to the grievances—specific accusations of misconduct by the king—and he needs to go in hot.

★ UNITED STATES OF AMERICA ★

The first known use of "United States of America" is in a January 2, 1776, letter written by one member of George Washington's staff to another. The writer, Stephen Moylan, was an Irish immigrant who replaced the letter's recipient, Joseph Reed, as Washington's senior aide-de-camp while Reed was away. Moylan soon took over that position permanently. Reed later was the first man to suspect wrongdoing by the traitor Benedict Arnold.

THE GRIEVANCES

There are twenty-seven grievances—charges against King George III—and they take up more than two-thirds of the Declaration. All of them reflect the world after the French and Indian War, when Britain had begun paying more attention to the colonies, and trying to extract more money from them, too. Some clues to Jefferson's thinking can be found in his *A Summary View of the Rights of British America*, published in 1774. It includes eight grievances against the king that he repurposed in the Declaration of Independence, as well as material from his preamble for Virginia's state constitution.

The grievances are notable for three things. First, they were made against the king, not Parliament. In 1774, the First Continental Congress had decreed that colonists were not under Parliament's control. Therefore, the king was the link connecting colonists to the mother country. Attacking the king would break that last bond—and Jefferson is breaking it.

Second, the accusations are overblown and exaggerated, and they sometimes ignore inconvenient facts. That makes sense for an argument—Jefferson was making as strong a case for independence as possible, aimed at the real audience of the document: the

American people. And he picks up steam as he goes along, creating a dramatic arc within the Declaration.

Third, Jefferson isn't very specific about the events that prompted each grievance. Historians and readers today still puzzle over precisely what he meant, and eighteenth-century readers wondered, too. Former Massachusetts governor Thomas Hutchinson, a Loyalist (supporter of the British government), criticized the first grievance as ". . . without any particulars to support it," saying that made it "fit enough to be placed at the head of a list of imaginary grievances." A British lawyer named John Lind wrote a pamphlet rebutting the Declaration soon after its publication, where he said that the sheer number of complaints was proof of their weakness. He wrote that the grievances tried "to supply by numbers, what they wanted in weight; to confuse where they could not hope to convince."

But Jefferson's technique was effective, as the vagueness gave the impression that there may have been more violations of colonists' liberty than people realized. The result: You might not know what each item in the list meant, but the sum total made you mad. The grievances weren't meant to explain which events had pushed colonists toward independence. Rather, they were meant to justify independence: The king was a tyrant, so the revolution was legitimate. Jefferson knew what he was doing, and he succeeded.

1. ***He has refused his Assent to Laws, the most wholesome and necessary for the public good.***

DECODED **The King has refused to approve laws we need.**

This complaint is an irritated slap at British micromanagement. The internal laws made by colonial legislatures required the king's approval. Often, the king had withheld his assent from these laws—in essence vetoing them. This was even more galling because the king no longer vetoed acts of Parliament. Colonists were being treated as second-class citizens compared to their British brethren.

2. ***He has forbidden his Governors to pass Laws of immediate and pressing importance, unless suspended in their operation till his Assent should be obtained; and when so suspended, he has utterly neglected to attend to them.***

DECODED **He has forbidden colonial governors from passing important and necessary laws unless they're prevented from going into effect until they get his okay; and once those laws have been passed and put on hold, he doesn't bother to deal with them.**

This charge is similar to Grievance 1 in focusing on how laws were passed and implemented. Colonial laws were unable to go into effect until the king had given his assent, or agreement. Given the time required to travel between the colonies and Britain—a four-week journey by ship to go just one way—the delay could be significant. Four Virginia laws from 1770 took Britain almost three years to think over. Then they set one law aside to wait for more information! Parliament claimed it needed to suspend laws precisely because transatlantic communication took so long; suspension was an alternative to overturning a law months or even years after it had taken effect. But to colonists, having their laws suspended when Parliament's laws couldn't be paused was again evidence that they held a lower class of citizenship.

3. ***He has refused to pass other Laws for the accommodation of large districts of people, unless those people would relinquish the right of Representation in the Legislature, a right inestimable to them and formidable to tyrants only.***

DECODED He has refused to pass laws letting new settlements have representation in their colonial legislatures. Representation is a right of great importance to those settlers, and only a tyrant needs to prevent it.

To the colonists, it seemed obvious that as their territory expanded, new communities should have political rights, but England blocked new settlements from electing their own representatives to colonial assemblies. Former Massachusetts governor Thomas Hutchinson thought his colony was the main complainant here.

This grievance is a reminder that the Declaration accommodated the complaints of thirteen colonies. Each colony had different experiences, which may explain the number of charges building the case against the king. Some complaints were specific to just one colony, but their inclusion is a show of solidarity: What had offended one colony now offended all.

4. ***He has called together legislative bodies at places unusual, uncomfortable, and distant from the depository of their public Records, for the sole purpose of fatiguing them into compliance with his measures.***

DECODED **He has made legislatures gather at places that aren't their regular meeting spots and which are uncomfortable and a long way from where their records are kept—just to exhaust them into going along with what he wants.**

Britain dissolved the Virginia legislature in 1765 and the Virginia, Massachusetts, and South Carolina legislatures in 1768. Massachusetts Governor Francis Bernard required the legislature to meet in Cambridge (instead of in Boston) when it was suspended in 1768, and Governor Thomas Gage moved the legislature even farther in 1774—to Salem, which made the trip about four times longer.

John Lind, the British lawyer who rebutted Jefferson's "audacious paper," found this allegation "truly ridiculous." He said, "At the first blush it looks as if inserted by an enemy . . . to throw an air of ridicule on the declaration in general." The colonial legislators were only "compelled to sit on strange seats," Lind said. How bad was that, really? An adult should be able to handle a new chair. But to the colonists, changing the legislature's meeting place was evidence of British duplicity and injustice. It seemed as if British rulers were deliberately making it difficult for Americans to govern themselves.

5. *He has dissolved Representative Houses repeatedly, for opposing with manly firmness his invasions on the rights of the people.*

DECODED **He has dissolved legislatures that tried to prevent him from stepping on people's rights.**

If a colonial assembly acted in ways that displeased a royal governor, the governor could "prorogue" the assembly, which meant sending all the representatives home for a while. Proroguing let the governor flex his power, and with any luck, the legislators would cool down before they reassembled. A governor could also dissolve the legislature, which actually ended the terms of all the existing representatives. Colonists might then elect new representatives who were more cooperative toward the Crown.

The king had approved the suspension of the New York assembly in 1767 for refusing to comply with the Quartering Act and of the Massachusetts assembly in 1768 after it opposed the Townshend Acts. The colonists saw this as denying them an operating government after they merely stood up for their own rights. But to the British, this grievance used actions the king had taken to suppress a revolt to justify having started the revolt in the first place. It's twisty logic on Jefferson's part, but good propaganda.

6. ***He has refused for a long time, after such dissolutions, to cause others to be elected; whereby the Legislative powers, incapable of Annihilation, have returned to the People at large for their exercise; the State remaining in the mean time exposed to all the dangers of invasion from without, and convulsions within.***

DECODED After dissolving colonial legislatures, the king has taken a long time to hold elections for new representatives. Since the power to pass laws doesn't just disappear, during those times the power has gone back to the people, but the colony has been left vulnerable to invasion and internal chaos in the meantime.

This again likely refers to the 1768 suspension of the Massachusetts legislature. After the Declaration was published, Thomas Hutchinson pointed out that the colony had been without a government for fewer than three months, but that missed the larger point: Denying colonists local government at all was a violation of their rights.

7. ***He has endeavoured to prevent the population of these States; for that purpose obstructing the Laws for Naturalization of Foreigners; refusing to pass others to encourage their migrations hither, and raising the conditions of new Appropriations of Lands.***

DECODED He's tried to keep the states from being settled with more people. To further that aim, he's blocked the legal process for foreigners to become citizens, refused to pass laws encouraging immigration, and made it harder for everyone to get land.

In the early 1770s, the British government considered preventing further emigration to the American colonies because the exodus of people from the British Isles had become so great. As an example, in the entire decade of the 1750s, approximately 14,200 people immigrated to North America from northeastern Ireland. But in only the first five years of the 1770s, 13,200 people immigrated from that area—nearly as many people in half the time.

Parliament did not actually pass laws preventing emigration. But in 1773, it did revoke the Naturalization Act of 1740. That act had made it easy to become a citizen of the colonies as long as you were Protestant. Now it would be harder to attract new residents to the colonies, Jefferson argued, and that would hurt their development. People who were partway through the immigration process would be stuck.

The bigger issue underlying this grievance was the wildly unpopular Proclamation Line of 1763, drawn across the crest of the Appalachian Mountains after the French and Indian War. British colonists couldn't colonize any land west of the line—essentially the Ohio River Valley, where western Pennsylvania, West Virginia, Ohio, Indiana, Illinois, Kentucky, and Tennessee are today—and those who were already past it had to pull back. The line was intended to prevent trespass on Indigenous lands that the British had taken from the French, which could provoke another war, but it also kept colonists from acquiring profitable farmland that could reduce their dependence on commerce with Britain.

8. ***He has obstructed the Administration of Justice, by refusing his Assent to Laws for establishing Judiciary powers.***

DECODED **He hasn't let us set up courts, which has prevented justice from being served.**

This charge is the first to complain about interference with the judicial branch; the first seven dealt with legislative issues. Grievance 8 grew out of a conflict in North Carolina. The assembly had passed a bill setting up superior courts, which included a clause that made it easier for colonists to file claims against people who lived in Britain. Under existing English law, a person who wanted to claim money they were owed had to file a claim in the debtor's district. Americans who had a beef with British landowners would have to spend a lot of time and money filing a claim in a location convenient for the British owner, and the North Carolina clause addressed that issue. The Crown thought this clause violated the law, and when the colony refused to strike it, its superior courts were closed in 1773.

The royal governor tried to set the courts back up, and he had the king's okay to do so. But the colonial assembly then declined to pay the judges or recognize the Crown's right to establish the courts. North Carolina may have felt it needed to hold the line on English control over colonial justice. Still, if Jefferson had been completely candid about precisely who had obstructed the administration of justice here, it wouldn't have helped his case against the king.

9. ***He has made Judges dependent on his Will alone, for the tenure of their offices, and the amount and payment of their salaries.***

DECODED He's made the judges dependent on him for their jobs and how much and whether they get paid.

The king issued an order in December 1761 forbidding colonists from giving judges a set term in office. Instead, judges were to serve at "the pleasure of the Crown," which meant "Annoy George III, get fired." The order was to be permanent. This was another measure that seemed to give colonists second-class citizenship: In Britain, for decades, judges had served as long as they maintained good behavior. Furthermore, the Townshend Acts of 1767 let Britain start paying judges' salaries, which became another way to increase the judges' reliance on the Crown. An independent judiciary was crucial for a free people, but colonists didn't have one.

10. ***He has erected a multitude of New Offices, and sent hither swarms of Officers to harrass our people, and eat out their substance.***

DECODED He has created a huge number of new officials, who bother us and cost us money.

The American Board of Customs Commissioners, headquartered in Boston, tried to root out the smuggling of goods to the colonies and make colonists pay tariffs (taxes on goods entering the colonies) instead. This was enormously unpopular, as smuggling was a significant part of the colonial economy.

11. ***He has kept among us, in times of peace, Standing Armies without the Consent of our legislatures.***

DECODED He has kept an army here during peacetime and without permission from our legislatures.

The king sent troops to Boston in 1768 to enforce British law and protect British officials. Conflicts between the soldiers and the colonists led to the Boston Massacre in 1770. More troops arrived in 1774 when

General Thomas Gage, commander in chief of British forces in America, was made governor of troublesome Massachusetts and established a military government there. To the British, it made perfect sense to send soldiers to protect their economic interests and the customs officials who enforced them.

The colonists, however, thought that given the ongoing relative peace with Indigenous nations and with the French gone, there was no need for a standing army in the colonies. The military wasn't there to protect them; it was there to control them. The presence of the king's troops would lead directly to the quartering conflict seen in Grievance 14.

12. *He has affected to render the Military independent of and superior to the Civil power.*

DECODED He has made the military not subject to, and more powerful than, the nonmilitary government authorities.

This grievance goes hand in glove with the one above. George III had sent an army to occupy Massachusetts and replaced the civilian governor with a military officer (Thomas Gage). That was offensive enough to get two grievances—and when the Constitution was written eleven years later, the Framers wrote it into law that the commander in chief would be a civilian.

13. ***He has combined with others to subject us to a jurisdiction foreign to our constitution, and unacknowledged by our laws; giving his Assent to their Acts of pretended Legislation:***

DECODED **Along with others, the king has put us under a power that our laws don't recognize; and agreed to illegitimate laws:**

Both the "others" and "jurisdiction foreign to our constitution" here refer to Parliament; colonists continued to claim that they were not under its rule ("unacknowledged by our laws"). "Pretended legislation" may have referred in general to taxes imposed by Parliament, to which King George III gave his assent, or targeted the Board of Trade, which enforced the new taxes and trade laws. Or Jefferson may have been taking a swipe at the Declaratory Act of 1766, in which Parliament claimed that it had the right to rule for the colonies "in all cases whatsoever," infuriating colonists. But Jefferson then gets pretty explicit about what those illegitimate laws are, as he uses this grievance to introduce the charges that follow. Note that the format changes from "He has" to "For. . . " and stays that way until the final few grievances, when Jefferson cranks his case up.

14. ***For Quartering large bodies of armed troops among us:***

DECODED **For housing large numbers of soldiers in our homes:**

Once the king had sent troops to the colonies (Grievance 11), they needed housing, or "quartering." General Thomas Gage, the commander of British forces in the colonies, wanted to reduce the expense of maintaining his troops, so he asked Parliament to allow them to be put up in private homes. British citizens had been guaranteed freedom from having a soldier live in their house since 1628, and violation of that right would outrage any Englishman or -woman. Parliament had a sharp debate over Gage's request, and after Benjamin Franklin intervened, a watered-down Quartering Act passed in 1765. The colonies had to provide quarters for British troops, but they didn't have to be in private homes. (The soldiers could be housed in empty buildings, for example.) Colonists *did* have to provide the things that a home would have, among them bedding, candles, and beer. All of this would be at the colonists' own expense, and they couldn't turn away any soldiers who were assigned to their property. When New York refused to provide some of the goods—including the beer—Parliament suspended its legislature until it changed its mind.

The issue didn't end there. A second Quartering Act passed in 1774—one of the Intolerable Acts—allowed troops to be quartered in private homes. Like the other Intolerable Acts, it was an affront to the colonies. These acts outraged the colonists and led directly to the Third Amendment to the US Constitution, which outlaws quartering troops in private homes: "No Soldier shall, in time of peace be quartered in any house, without the consent of the Owner, nor in time of war, but in a manner to be prescribed by law."

15. ***For protecting them, by a mock Trial, from punishment for any Murders which they should commit on the Inhabitants of these States:***

DECODED For rigging criminal trials so British soldiers aren't punished for murdering people here:

The Administration of Justice Act (1774) let British troops accused of crimes against Americans be tried in England, with a British judge and jury, where it would be very difficult for Americans to gather witnesses and make an effective case. The law passed four years after the Boston Massacre, in which British troops had shot and killed local citizens. Colonists thought the Administration of Justice Act gave soldiers, whom they saw as occupiers, the license to commit crimes with little chance for the colonists to get justice. They called it the Murder Act.

16. *For cutting off our Trade with all parts of the world:*

DECODED **For preventing us from trading with other nations:**

Britain had moved to dominate commerce with the colonies from the mid-1600s; it had been tenacious in its efforts to profit from colonial trade. It had also been specific; for example, in 1732 it forbade colonists from manufacturing or exporting hats, which helped British hatmakers at the expense of the colonial economy. But colonial smuggling was widespread and British officials in the colonies often turned a blind eye to it—until the 1760s, and the end of salutary neglect.

Jefferson doesn't specify an act here, but several British laws qualify as cutting off colonial trade, such as the Boston Port Act (1774), passed after the Boston Tea Party. It closed the port of Boston, a huge blow to Massachusetts, since its economy relied heavily on shipping. Parliament imposed it because ". . . dangerous commotions and insurrections have been fomented and raised in the town of Boston . . . by divers ill-affected persons . . ." It was clearly an economic punishment for a political rebellion.

Furthermore, in March 1775, Parliament declared that four colonies—Massachusetts, Connecticut, New Hampshire, and Rhode Island—couldn't trade with any nation but Britain. A month later it added Pennsylvania, New Jersey, Maryland, Virginia, and South Carolina to the list when it learned they were participating in boycotts of British goods.

But Jefferson surely had the most recent and most extreme possible law in mind when he wrote this: the December 1775 Prohibitory Act. The Prohibitory Act didn't regulate or tax trade between Britain and the colonies. It simply cut all trade off. Americans couldn't trade with Britain *or* with foreign nations, either. Colonial ships were classified as enemy vessels, and the British navy was empowered to seize them. The navy could auction off any captured ships and cargo, with the money going to the Crown. All of this meant the colonists weren't free to buy or sell the goods they wanted, and any ships or property on the seas could be taken at any time.

Trade rights, and British restrictions, were an important cause of the Revolution. Parliament acted again and again over more than a century to ensure that most profits went to Britain, not the colonies. For colonists it wasn't just about the money, although that was important. Britain was engaging in unfair trade practices that penalized them. If they were truly British citizens, how was that acceptable?

17. *For imposing Taxes on us without our Consent:*

DECODED For taxing us without our agreement:

This was both the shortest grievance and the heart of the matter. Parliament had been relentless about trying to recover its expenses in the French and Indian War, which it felt it had waged in part for the defense of the colonists. How could they fail to pay their fair share to reduce Britain's debt?

Parliament had imposed tariffs before—the Sugar Act of 1764, for example, attempted to enforce a three-pence-per-gallon tax on all imported molasses. But in 1765, it passed the Stamp Act, followed by the Townshend Acts in 1767. Both taxed *internal* colonial commerce—sales made within the colonies' borders. The colonists were outraged to be taxed by a legislature in which they had no representatives, and their rallying cry became "No taxation without representation."

This wasn't just a matter of money; they had rights as citizens and deserved to have a say in what taxes were passed. The feeling was strong enough that the US Constitution requires all money bills to begin in the House of Representatives, which is elected directly by the people. (Senators were originally elected by state legislators.) Given how central the cause of taxation without representation was, it's almost shocking that Jefferson didn't list it later in the Declaration. But by the time he was writing, the king had committed even greater offenses—he had waged war on his people.

18. *For depriving us in many cases, of the benefits of Trial by Jury:*

DECODED For often denying us jury trials:

The Sugar Act of 1764 included strict rules of enforcement. Ship captains had to get papers listing their cargoes before loading or unloading and were subject to prosecution if they were lax with the paperwork. If captains were prosecuted, their trials could be moved to a vice-admiralty court on the whim of British customs officials. Unlike colonial courts, vice-admiralty courts didn't use juries. The judge who decided the case and chose the punishment was a Crown appointee. The defendant was presumed guilty; if he managed to prove himself innocent, he still couldn't recover damages, or even expenses.

This wasn't just an enormous pain for individuals or a blow to colonial commerce. It was a tool of coercion and control. And as far as colonists were concerned, it violated traditional English rights. In 1215, King John had ruled so badly that the barons wrote down their rights and forced the king to sign a document guaranteeing them. This charter, known as the Magna Carta, was foundational to English liberty, and it included the right for a man to have "lawful judgement of his equals"—a trial by jury. By denying colonists that right, the British were saying they were not full citizens.

19. ***For transporting us beyond Seas to be tried for pretended offences:***

DECODED For shipping us overseas for trial on made-up charges:

In June 1772, a British schooner called the *Gaspée* was patrolling the coast of Rhode Island to suppress smuggling. Its commander, Lieutenant William Dudingston, made himself very unpopular with the colonists—which became a problem when he ran the *Gaspée* onto a sandbar. That night a band of colonists rowed out and boarded the *Gaspée*. When Dudingston tried to resist, they shot him in the groin. Then they took everyone off the ship and set it on fire.

Parliament was outraged. This was a royal ship performing its duties, however much the colonists didn't like it. The commission investigating the *Gaspée* Affair was given the power to send suspects to England for trial. That was menacing news for potential defendants—especially as it would make it impossible for them to produce witnesses on their behalf. The Crown offered a five-hundred-pound reward for turning in the culprits but got no takers. The only one punished was Dudingston, who was court-martialed for losing the *Gaspée*. While no colonist seems to have been sent to trial in England after the *Gaspée* Affair or in later conflicts, the possibility was still shocking. The injustice was written into law in 1774 by the Administration of Justice Act, part of the Intolerable Acts.

This issue led directly to the provision in the US Constitution that an accused person's trial must be held in the "state and district" where the crime occurred.

20. ***For abolishing the free System of English Laws in a neighbouring Province, establishing therein an Arbitrary government, and enlarging its Boundaries so as to render it at once an example and fit instrument for introducing the same absolute rule into these Colonies:***

DECODED For not using English laws in a neighboring colony, setting up an unfair government there, and then making that colony bigger, modeling how to bring unjust rule to our colonies:

The "neighbouring Province" was Quebec (now a part of Canada), which had been taken from France in the French and Indian War. The Quebec Act was the fifth of the Intolerable Acts of 1774. Parliament extended the border of Quebec down to the Ohio River, into the area that's now Ohio, Indiana, and Illinois. That crushed the dream of westward expansion for British colonists. That the fruitful Ohio River Valley was given to French-speaking Catholics, who had recently been Britain's enemies, made it even more bitter.

Parliament was trying to win the allegiance of people who had been French citizens. The Quebec Act allowed them to practice Catholicism, and, as English settlers weren't flooding the area, it kept some French law in place. This is the "arbitrary government" mentioned above. Congressional delegates thought Parliament's failure to establish an elected assembly for Quebec was an abuse of power. Jefferson speculates that Quebec could provide a model: Would Britain try to govern the thirteen English colonies without popularly elected legislatures? Given how much trouble colonial assemblies had been causing, it might have been a tempting thought.

21. ***For taking away our Charters, abolishing our most valuable Laws, and altering fundamentally the Forms of our Governments:***

DECODED For repealing the documents that founded our colonies and our most important laws, and significantly changing the way our government is structured:

In the Massachusetts Government Act, one of the five Intolerable Acts of 1774, Parliament revoked Massachusetts's 1691 charter. Instead, Massachusetts got a military government headed by General Thomas Gage. Popularly elected officials were replaced by ones appointed by England, and sheriffs could choose jurors for trials, further limiting the right to a trial by your peers. And New England towns, which governed themselves through town meetings, were limited to one meeting per year, effectively making it impossible for local elected governments to function at all.

22. ***For suspending our own Legislatures, and declaring themselves invested with power to legislate for us in all cases whatsoever.***

DECODED For preventing our assemblies from meeting, and claiming that Parliament can make all our laws.

As mentioned earlier, the royal governors suspended colonial assemblies when the legislatures didn't behave, and Parliament backed them up on it. Depriving people of their elected legislatures denied them the right of self-governance.

The last clause—"in all cases whatsoever"—is a bitter reference to Parliament's Declaratory Act. In 1766, Parliament repealed the Stamp Act because it was impossible to enforce in the face of colonial outrage. The same day, it passed the Declaratory Act, claiming the colonies were under British rule and reasserting Parliament's right to legislate for the colonies "in all cases whatsoever." (That is, not just in foreign policy and trade, but also in internal issues.) It was a uniquely irritating document, and every colonist would recognize Jefferson's wording here, flung back in the king's face.

23. *He has abdicated Government here, by declaring us out of his Protection and waging War against us.*

DECODED **The king has failed to lead by announcing he won't protect us and by attacking us.**

This grievance lands like a hammer blow because it was both shocking and true. George III had opened a new session of Parliament in October 1775 with an address that launched straight into the colonial issue.

He referred to the colonies' "subordinate relation to Great-Britain" and said they "now openly avow their revolt, hostility, and rebellion." The king went on to say, "The rebellious war now . . . is manifestly carried on for the purpose of establishing an independent empire." The Second Continental Congress must have been startled to read this when the news arrived in January 1776; George III declared the colonies wanted to be independent before Congress itself did.

In his speech, George finally announced it was time "to put a speedy end to these disorders by the most decisive exertions[.] For this purpose, I have increased my naval establishment, and greatly augmented my land forces . . ." It was a declaration of war—on his own colonies. And indeed the king's forces had already fought the colonists at Lexington and Concord in April 1775, and at Bunker Hill in June.

If George III considered the thirteen colonies to be English, he was waging war on his people, which justified their revolt. If he considered them a foreign nation, he was acknowledging their independence. Either way, what obligation did the colonists have to a king who attacked them?

24. ***He has plundered our seas, ravaged our Coasts, burnt our towns, and destroyed the lives of our people.***

DECODED He has attacked our ships and coasts, burned our towns, and killed colonists.

Jefferson was probably thinking of three cities in particular when he wrote this grievance: Charlestown, Massachusetts; Falmouth, Massachusetts; and Norfolk, Virginia. Charlestown burned during the Battle of Bunker Hill in June 1775 when British ships fired hot cannonballs into the town, setting its wooden buildings on fire.

Falmouth was burned in retaliation for colonial attacks on British ships. Captain Henry Mowat sailed into the harbor, gave the townspeople two hours to evacuate, and then lit the town up with incendiary cannonballs. Landing parties set fire to buildings that weren't already ablaze. The attack left about a thousand civilians homeless.

Norfolk is the most interesting case. It was strategically important for defense, the most populous city in Virginia and a Loyalist stronghold. After losing a battle that December, British troops retreated to Norfolk. Lacking enough men to hold the town, the soldiers fled onto the British warships in the harbor and even some commercial vessels. Conditions on board the ships were crowded and unpleasant, and the colonists decided to stand guard and make the soldiers stay there. Then they goaded the troops by changing their guard on the waterfront where the British would see them. In case the point was lost, they also made obscene gestures.

On January 1, 1776, after colonists refused to sell provisions to the British ships, the British fleet fired on the waterfront and sent parties ashore to set fire to some of the buildings. Colonial troops got drunk and torched the rest of Norfolk's buildings, with the full approval of their officers, as burning the city down was considered preferable to letting it fall into British hands. So while the British did bear responsibility for starting the blaze, colonists did most of the damage.

Jefferson knew all of that context. But he also recognized good propaganda when he saw it. News of the burning of Norfolk arrived in Philadelphia at the same time that Thomas Paine's *Common Sense* began to circulate, and Norfolk's destruction outraged colonists. For American readers of Grievance 24, Norfolk would have sprung immediately to mind.

25. ***He is at this time transporting large Armies of foreign Mercenaries to compleat the works of death, desolation and tyranny, already begun with circumstances of Cruelty & perfidy scarcely paralleled in the most barbarous ages, and totally unworthy the Head of a civilized nation.***

DECODED At this very moment, he is sending large numbers of soldiers hired from other countries to complete the process of killing us and ending our liberty. This is so horrible that it's hard to find anything like it in history, and it's unbefitting the ruler of an advanced country.

Hiring mercenaries (foreign soldiers) to fight wars was a common practice in Europe, but to the colonists, it was an incredibly dirty move. Their own king sent troops against them, and the soldiers weren't even their countrymen!

In the draft that the Committee of Five eventually presented to Congress, Jefferson wrote near the end that British citizens were allowing their king "to send over not only soldiers of our common blood, but Scotch & foreign mercenaries to invade and deluge us in blood." His draft of this twenty-fifth grievance contained the same phrase, that "Scotch" and other mercenaries were about to unleash "death, desolation and tyranny." Two members of the Second Continental Congress had been born in Scotland: John Witherspoon and James Wilson. Witherspoon had emigrated only eight years before and apparently objected to singling out Scots. The offending word was struck from both places.

Why did Jefferson mention Scottish people at all? British military recruitment efforts after April 1775 found few takers in England and Ireland, but the people of Scotland were so poor that several thousand Highlanders signed up. They weren't enough to fill the ranks, however, so George III tried to secure the return of a Scottish mercenary brigade from Holland, which rebuffed the effort, and then get Russian soldiers from Catherine the Great. When that, too, failed, he signed troops from a number of German states, including Hesse. Today we often call these mercenaries "Hessians," referring to troops from any of the German states. While Congress debated the Declaration, mercenaries were already crossing the Atlantic.

26. ***He has constrained our fellow Citizens taken Captive on the high Seas to bear Arms against their Country, to become the executioners of their friends and Brethren, or to fall themselves by their Hands.***

DECODED **He has forced captured colonial sailors to fight against the colonies, where they either must kill their friends and brothers, or be killed by them.**

In December 1775, after receiving the Olive Branch Petition, Parliament passed the Prohibitory Act. It authorized the Royal Navy not only to seize colonial ships, but to "impress" their sailors, forcing them to sail for the British. While impressment was a serious issue, the brother-against-brother scenario Jefferson envisions doesn't seem to have occurred often. In reality, American captives usually preferred staying in prison over service in the Royal Navy.

When England continued the practice of impressment after the Revolution, it became a major cause of the War of 1812.

27. ***He has excited domestic insurrections amongst us, and has endeavoured to bring on the inhabitants of our frontiers, the merciless Indian Savages, whose known rule of warfare, is an undistinguished destruction of all ages, sexes and conditions.***

DECODED He has started revolts, and tried to have us attacked by the people who live at the edge of our territories—Indigenous people, who kill regardless of their victims' age, sex, or health.

The charge of "exciting domestic insurrections" implies that the British encouraged revolts of enslaved people. In November 1775, Virginia Governor Lord Dunmore offered freedom to enslaved people in exchange for joining the British forces. Eventually about eight hundred Black men served in a segregated regiment.

The British also had Indigenous allies, and later encouraged Indigenous attacks on colonists, launched from western forts and trading posts. While the colonists were outraged by this, most violence on the frontier was the result of their own westward push, not incitement by the king or Parliament.

The offensive language regarding Indigenous people here may have been especially harsh not just because the Declaration functioned as propaganda for white colonists, but also because Jefferson served on a committee for the Second Continental Congress that investigated the mistreatment of colonial prisoners in Canada by Indigenous fighters. Whatever he learned there likely hardened his attitude toward the original inhabitants of the continent.

In his draft, Jefferson ends the grievances section with climactic final charges, including an indictment of the king for blocking colonial efforts to tax and end the transatlantic slave trade. The passage was eventually deleted, but it reads:

> **28.** ***He has waged cruel war against human nature itself, violating its most sacred rights of life & liberty, in the persons of a distant people who never offended him, captivating & carrying them into slavery in another hemisphere, or to incur miserable death in their transportation thither. This piratical warfare, the opprobrium of*** **infidel** ***powers is the warfare of the*** **Christian** ***king of Great Britain. Determined***

to keep open a market in which MEN should be bought & sold, he has prostituted his negative for suppressing every legislative attempt to prohibit or restrain this execrable commerce and that this assemblage of horrors might want no fact of distinguished die, he is now exciting those very people to rise in arms among us, and to purchase that liberty of which he *has deprived them, by murdering people among whom* he *also obtruded them; thus paying off former crimes committed against the liberties of one people, with crimes which he urges them to commit against the* lives *of another.*

DECODED The king has attacked humanity itself and the basic rights of life and freedom, by capturing people who never did anything to him, and enslaving them in another part of the world, or causing their horrifying deaths on the way there. This is shameful when done by *non-Christian* rulers, but this is being done by the *Christian* king of Great Britain. To keep markets for enslaved people open, he's misused his right to veto laws by quashing every law trying to end or restrict this trade. And to make this horrible situation as bad as possible, he's now trying to get those same enslaved people to rebel and regain the liberty that *he* took from them by killing the people among whom *he* put them. In that way he makes amends for taking one people's *liberty* by urging them to take another people's *lives*.

This paragraph is often incorrectly described as Jefferson's call to end slavery, which in 1776 was legal in all colonies (although the great majority of enslaved people lived in the southern colonies, from Maryland to Georgia). By some historians' estimates, at least forty of the fifty-six signers of the Declaration enslaved people, including three members of the Committee of Five: Benjamin Franklin, Robert Livingston, and Jefferson. Jefferson was aware of the awful irony of enslaving people himself while writing that all men are created equal, and some attempts to end the trade may have been a recognition that slavery violated "sacred rights of life & liberty."

But this paragraph targeted only the transatlantic slave trade, not slavery as an institution. Jefferson and his fellow Southern plantation owners had economic reasons for wanting to end the slave trade: For some colonies, like Virginia, continuing the international slave trade would drive down the price of enslaved people already in the colony, decreasing the wealth of men like Jefferson. He also ended the passage with a complaint about the British offer to free enslaved men who would join the British to fight their enslavers.

The idea that King George III was personally responsible for the North American slave trade was ridiculous; after all, enslaved Africans had first reached England's North American colonies in 1619, well over a century before the king's birth. And while Jefferson blamed the king for the trade in human beings, the British saw the *colonists* as the enslavers. British ships had delivered people in chains to the colonial shore, but Americans had adopted and perpetuated the institution.

John Adams liked this paragraph, but even he thought it was an overreach. The entire passage was struck during the Congressional editing process.

THE FORMAL DECLARATION OF INDEPENDENCE

The formal Declaration of Independence doesn't declare principles, like the Preamble, or make accusations, like the Grievances; it takes action. This is the section that declares the United States of America to be a free and independent nation.

> *In every stage of these Oppressions We have Petitioned for Redress in the most humble terms: Our repeated Petitions have been answered only by repeated injury. A Prince, whose character is thus marked by every act which may define a Tyrant, is unfit to be the ruler of a free people.*

DECODED Through all this ill treatment, we have respectfully asked for these abuses to end: Our requests have been met only with more abuse. A ruler who acts like a dictator isn't qualified to govern a free people.

And here it is—the move from wagging a finger at the king to saying he could no longer rule the American colonies. Some people consider this a twenty-eighth grievance, but it breaks the "He has" pattern of the previous charges. Jefferson's original wording said that "future ages will scarce believe" that one man could, over the course of only twelve years, enact "so many acts of tyranny." Congress cut the line, toning the passage down.

The right to petition the government—to make a request of the government, especially in writing—was found in the Magna Carta, that charter of English liberties. The right became even more important in the colonies, which could not petition in person because of the distance involved. For his part, King George III refused to read colonial petitions after 1766 because he thought the Declaratory Act of that year ended all doubt that Parliament had the right to make laws for, and tax, the colonies.

The colonists had continued to petition Parliament and the king anyway. In the Olive Branch Petition the previous year, Congress professed loyalty to the king and blamed his ministers for the problems. The petition urged George III to arrange an end to the hostilities. Instead he refused to read it, rejected the idea of reconciliation, and declared the colonists to be in revolt in his speech of October 1775.

The right to petition was so important that it is included in the First Amendment to the US Constitution.

Nor have We been wanting in attentions to our British brethren. We have warned them from time to time of attempts by their legislature to extend an unwarrantable jurisdiction over us. We have reminded them of the circumstances of our emigration and settlement here.

DECODED We've told British citizens about all this. We've told them about Parliament's unjustified attempts to rule over us. We reminded them how we came to move and live here.

Having blasted the king line after line, the Declaration now turns an unimpressed eye on British citizens, who had been told what was happening in the colonies but hadn't interceded. Colonial protests against the taxes levied by the Stamp Act and the Townshend Acts in the 1760s had been met with some support among British citizens; if they weren't much interested in colonial legislatures, they at least wanted to end boycotts of British goods. Colonists had hoped that support would continue. Because it didn't, the Declaration says, the Americans are cutting ties with king, Parliament—and the British people.

An "unwarrantable jurisdiction" meant that Parliament had no authority over the colonists, a point that colonists had made again and again.

The reminder of "the circumstances of our emigration and settlement here" is confusing to a modern eye. Jefferson maintained that the colonists immigrated at their own expense and on their own initiative and therefore owed nothing to Britain. Their allegiance to the king was shared by other British citizens, but that was the only link. The colonies were not a part of Britain, but a self-governing area under the Crown. Therefore, the colonial legislatures were equal to Parliament, and colonists should obey the laws of their own assemblies, which had legitimate authority over them. Jefferson strongly believed this. To the British, who saw colonies as subordinate by their very nature, it was ludicrous.

We have appealed to their native justice and magnanimity, and we have conjured them by the ties of our common kindred to disavow these usurpations, which, would inevitably interrupt our connections and correspondence. They too have been deaf to the voice of justice and of consanguinity. We must, therefore, acquiesce in the necessity, which denounces our Separation, and hold them, as we hold the rest of mankind, Enemies in War, in Peace Friends.

DECODED We have called on British citizens' sense of justice and our shared background to get them to reject these violations of our rights, which of course will cause problems in our relationships with them. They have ignored fairness and our common heritage. We thus reluctantly announce that we have severed ties and consider them, like everybody else, to be enemies in war, and friends in peacetime.

This claim that the British citizens had ignored the colonists was not entirely fair. The City of London petitioned the king on the colonists' behalf; news of the king's rejection of the petition arrived in late May 1776 and helped spur the cause of independence. But British citizens hadn't pressured Parliament consistently in the way colonists had hoped. And in the November 1774 election, British voters chose representatives who were hard-liners on the colonies, leading to further oppressions. Colonists were disillusioned.

"Denounce" in Jefferson's text means to formally announce the end of something, not to condemn it.

We, therefore, the Representatives of the united States of America, in General Congress, Assembled, appealing to the Supreme Judge of the world for the rectitude of our intentions, do, in the Name, and by Authority of the good People of these Colonies, solemnly publish and declare, That these United Colonies are, and of Right ought to be Free and Independent States; that they are Absolved from all Allegiance to the British Crown, and that all political connection between them and the State of Great Britain, is and ought to be totally dissolved; and that as Free and Independent States, they have full Power to levy War, conclude Peace, contract Alliances, establish Commerce, and to do all other Acts and Things which Independent States may of right do. And for the support of this Declaration, with a firm reliance on the protection of divine Providence, we mutually pledge to each other our Lives, our Fortunes and our sacred Honor.

DECODED We, the representatives of the United States of America, meeting as a whole Congress, and appealing to God for the goodness of our intentions, in the name and by the authority of the people of these colonies, announce that these united colonies are, and have a right to be, free and independent states. These states owe no loyalty to the British king, and all political connections between them and Great Britain are and should be gone. As free and independent states they can wage war, make peace, negotiate alliances, promote commerce, and wield all the powers of an independent nation. Relying on God's protection, we back up this Declaration with our lives, our property, and our sacred honor.

The Declaration is bookended by its claim to the right of revolution and its exercise of that right. Here at last, the colonies are "free and independent states." They claim all the powers of sovereign nations to conduct war, make alliances, further business and trade, and perform other acts in service to and at the direction of their citizens.

Here, too, is the last bit of the document's poetry, where language and thought transcend the historical moment. The Declaration didn't just announce a revolution; it announced the right of revolution. It didn't just rebuke a king; it rebuked the abuses of kings. In setting out principles of liberty and equality, Congress did what no body had done before: It announced the birth of a large, modern, unified nation in which the people would govern themselves. Officials would be elected and responsible to the public. Power would flow up from the people because it belonged to them.

Jefferson's appeal to the "Supreme Judge" sounds very much like John Locke, who said a legitimate rebellion against a tyrant was an "appeal to heaven." This conclusion was also an appeal to other nations—especially France—to recognize the United States as a new nation and support it in the conflict with the British that was surely to come.

Jefferson didn't need to bring the document back to the men sitting next to him in Congress, but the last line of the Declaration looks to them. That summer of 1776, they had sat together through miserable heat and suffered through twin plagues of flies and committee assignments. They could be hanged for treason for signing this document. Now they looked each other in the eye and gave a sober nod. Whatever happened next, this was a moment of heroism.

THE SIGNATURES

In the final text of the Declaration, Jefferson's words are followed by the signatures of fifty-six of the men who were part of the Second Continental Congress. John Hancock, a delegate from Massachusetts, signed first (and in the middle) because he was the president of the Congress. After that, delegates signed in a column on the right margin, following the custom of the time. Succeeding columns were to the left. (This is why the signatures on the left look ragged and misaligned; the last signers didn't need to leave room for others.) They signed by delegation, which means they were geographically clumped, signing from north to south. New Hampshire's delegates signed first; Georgia's last.

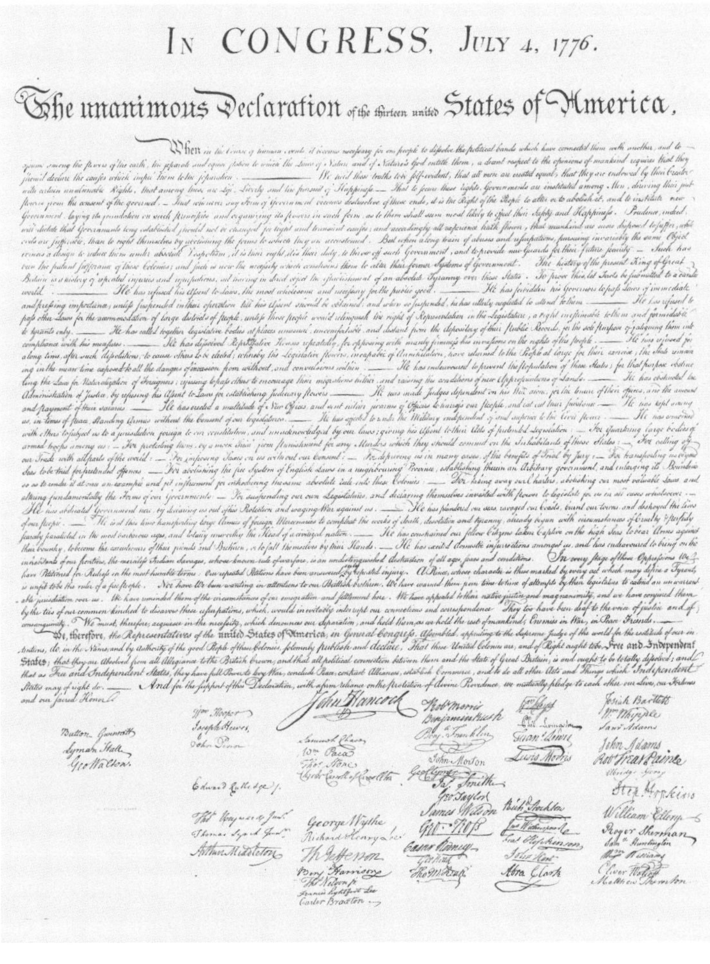

IN CONGRESS, JULY 4, 1776.

The unanimous Declaration of the thirteen united States of America,

GEORGIA

Button Gwinnett

Lyman Hall

George Walton

NORTH CAROLINA

William Hooper

Joseph Hewes

John Penn

SOUTH CAROLINA

Edward Rutledge

Thomas Heyward, Jr.

Thomas Lynch, Jr.

Arthur Middleton

MARYLAND

Samuel Chase

William Paca

Thomas Stone

Charles Carroll of Carrollton

VIRGINIA

George Wythe

Richard Henry Lee

Thomas Jefferson

Benjamin Harrison

Thomas Nelson, Jr.

Francis Lightfoot Lee

Carter Braxton

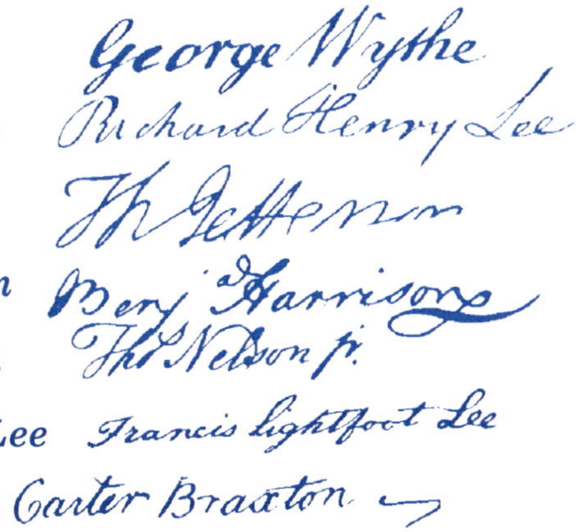

PENNSYLVANIA

Robert Morris

Benjamin Rush

Benjamin Franklin

John Morton

George Clymer

James Smith

George Taylor

James Wilson

George Ross

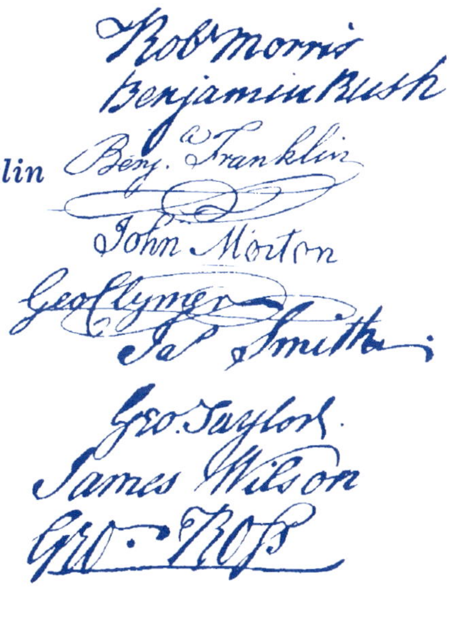

DELAWARE

Caesar Rodney
George Read
Thomas McKean

NEW YORK

William Floyd
Philip Livingston
Francis Lewis
Lewis Morris

NEW JERSEY

Richard Stockton
John Witherspoon
Francis Hopkinson
John Hart
Abraham Clark

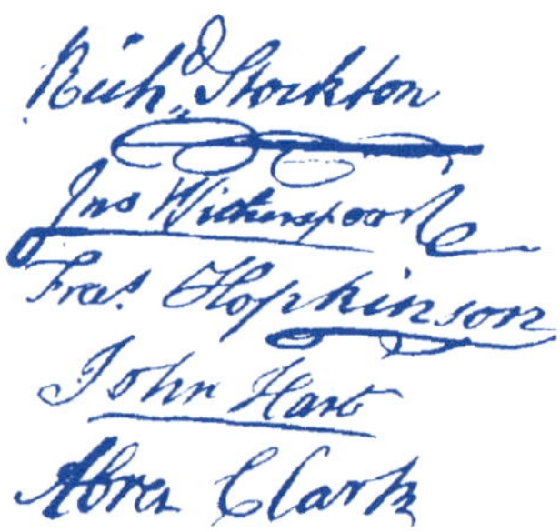

NEW HAMPSHIRE

Josiah Bartlett
William Whipple
Matthew Thornton

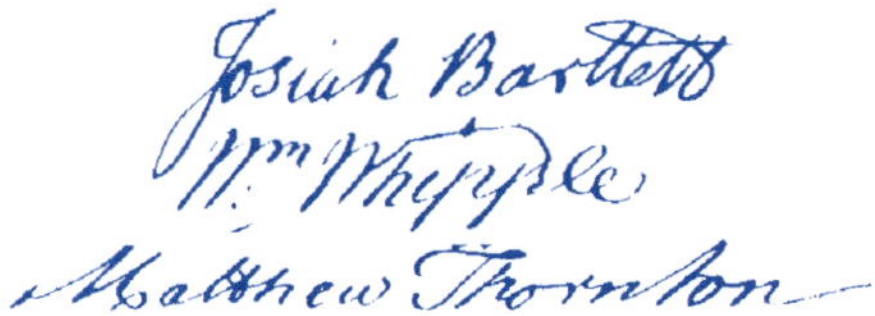

MASSACHUSETTS

John Hancock

Samuel Adams

John Adams

Robert Treat Paine

Elbridge Gerry

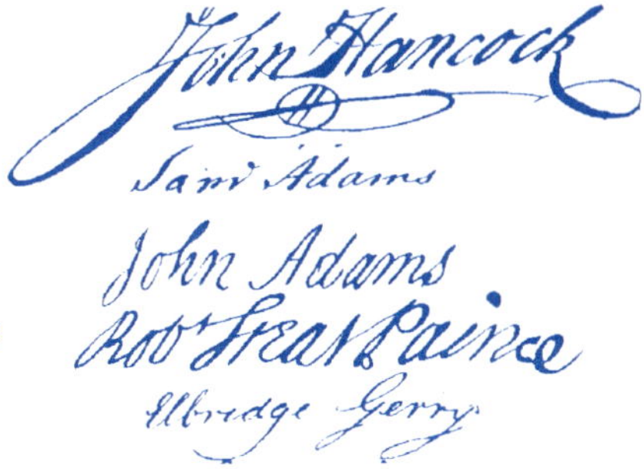

RHODE ISLAND

Stephen Hopkins

William Ellery

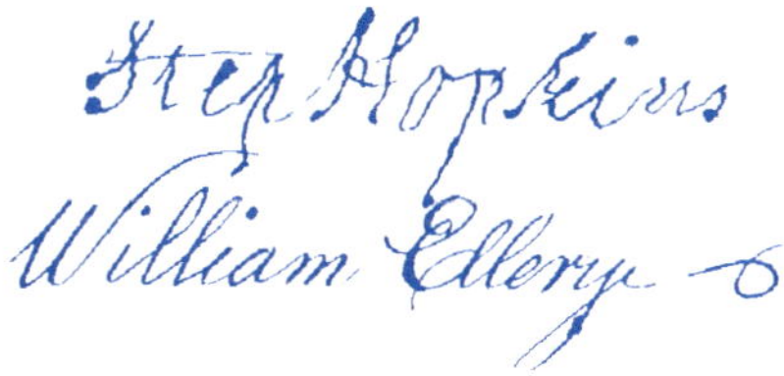

CONNECTICUT

Roger Sherman

Samuel Huntington

William Williams

Oliver Wolcott

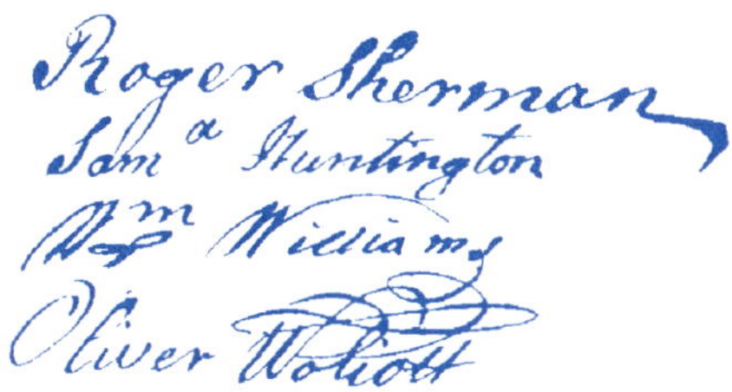

MANGLED AS IT IS

While Jefferson worked on the first draft of the Declaration, Congress took the Lee resolution up again. By June 28 every colony except New York had authorized its delegates to vote for independence. But the vote on June 28 failed, in part because Delaware had only two of its three delegates in the chamber, and they split. Delaware's missing delegate, Caesar Rodney, got news of the vote on July 1 and rode *eighty miles* overnight—more than double a hard day's ride. He arrived in Philadelphia on July 2, wet, muddy, and exhausted, but in time to vote for independence. Lee's resolution passed, affirming that "these United Colonies are, and of right, ought to be, Free and Independent States." This vote severed the United States from Britain.

But Congress still needed to make a proper announcement of that fact, and on June 28, 1776, the day of the failed vote, the Committee of Five presented the first draft of the Declaration to Congress.

The Committee had reviewed Jefferson's draft by this time. John Adams and Benjamin Franklin both made small edits before Roger Sherman and Robert Livingston saw it. Later Adams didn't remember the

Committee making many changes. He wrote that the draft contained "expressions which I would not have inserted if I had drawn it up, particularly that which called the king tyrant." But the draft was due. "We were all in haste. Congress was impatient." And so the Committee of Five put it before the Second Continental Congress.

The Congressional journal for June 28 said they "brought in a draught, which was read," without answering the tantalizing question: Who read it out loud? Jefferson was a remarkably inept public speaker who talked too quietly and tended to stare at his shoes. We don't know if he read it himself, but Jefferson's own copy contains quotation marks to indicate where a speaker would pause when reading out loud, or what phrases to emphasize. Their presence suggests he may have been the person to read the draft aloud to Congress. What a remarkable moment—Congress's best writer and worst speaker, holding the future in his hands: America would bow to no king.

After approving Lee's resolution on July 2, Congress worked as a committee of the whole to revise the Declaration. The delegates raked over Jefferson's words for the rest of the day. Finally they decided that they needed more time to edit the document. Jefferson must have been mortified.

The following two days Congress again dealt with urgent business—it had an army in the field—and then resolved into a committee of the whole to discuss the draft. The delegates left no official record of their changes or why they made them. Jefferson, logically enough, was the only delegate to keep detailed notes about congressional editing. He had reason to be irritated—they cut 25 percent of his draft. Many cuts deleted Jefferson's most extreme clauses. Others made the text more concise. Some were petty: His colleagues changed "neglected utterly" to "utterly neglected."

The most important cut, of course, was eliminating Jefferson's indictment of the slave trade (Grievance 28, as listed above). Jefferson's own notes say the passage was deleted "in complaisance to South Carolina and Georgia," and that some Northern states accepted the cut because while they didn't have many enslaved residents themselves, they were "pretty considerable carriers of them to others." In other words, New England shipping profited from the slave trade, too.

Congress added the clause that George III "excited domestic insurrections amongst us"—incited rebellions of enslaved people—to the twenty-seventh grievance, which blamed the king for turning Indigenous people against the colonists. It also incorporated two references to God, as Jefferson was a Deist and had mentioned only "nature's god." Thankfully they left his moving final sentence, pledging "our Lives, our Fortunes and our Sacred Honor."

Did Jefferson appreciate the editing help? Of course not. He was so convinced his version was better than the final document that he handwrote it several times and sent the copies to friends, hoping they'd tell him he was right and everyone else was wrong. (His friends tended to agree with him, even if history does not. Richard Henry Lee said he wished "the Manuscript had not been mangled as it is.") Jefferson later recalled that Franklin noticed his dismay as his colleagues imposed "these mutilations." Always the storyteller, Franklin told him about a hatmaker he knew who'd opened his own shop. He ordered a shop sign that read, "John Thompson, Hatter, makes and sells hats for ready money" beside a picture of a hat. His friends suggested cuts to the message until all that was left was "John Thomson" [sic] and the hat. Left unsaid was the point: This was the better sign. Franklin's sympathy may have taken the edge off the sting for Jefferson—but likely not by much.

On July 4, 1776, the committee of the whole announced that it had a Declaration, and the text was read aloud. Congress accepted it and ordered the document checked for accuracy and printed. As the Declaration wasn't fully signed until later, only the signatures of John Hancock, as Congress's president, and that of secretary Charles Thomson appear on the first published broadside. (Broadsides were a single sheet of paper printed on only one side, like a poster or flyer today.)

The congressional journal for July 19 says that after receiving New York's full approval of independence on July 9, the delegates decreed that "the Declaration passed on the 4th, be fairly engrossed on parchment, with the title and stile of 'The unanimous declaration of the thirteen United States of America,' and that the same, when engrossed, be signed by every member of Congress." And on August 2, "the declaration of independence being engrossed and compared was signed." ("Engrossed" means a final, official copy rendered in large, clear handwriting, ready to be signed.) Some members signed after August 2 for various reasons. For example, Thomas McKean left to serve as an officer in the war after voting for Lee's resolution and is believed to be the last delegate to sign, possibly as late as 1781.

A FRESH INCENTIVE

The Declaration functioned as a press release announcing independence to the country, especially the troops. After ordering the Declaration to be printed on July 4, Congress asked for copies to be "sent to the several assemblies, conventions and committees, or councils of safety, and to the several commanding officers of the continental troops; that it be proclaimed in each of the United States, and at the head of the army." The war wasn't going well, and colonial soldiers could use the boost to morale.

The news reached New York City on July 6. General George Washington received his copy from John Hancock, the president of Congress. The Continental Army was now fighting not just for their homes, but for their country. Washington called the Declaration a "fresh incentive," and indeed it led to spur-of-the-moment celebrations, many of which involved alcohol. Washington ordered troops in the city to the parade grounds at 6:00 p.m. on Tuesday, July 9, to hear the Declaration of Independence read out loud. After the reading, soldiers and townsfolk pulled down the gilded lead statue of George III on his horse. They cut off his head, his nose, and the laurels on his hair, and put the remnants of the head on a spike outside a tavern. Then some women melted the rest of the statue down to make musket balls for the Continental Army.

Throughout the colonies, civilians read the document in the newspapers or had a broadside read to them. Philadelphia held a public reading on July 8, and John Adams recorded that the "Bells rang all Day and almost all night." Readings continued throughout the colonies as copies of the document arrived, in some towns being read in several places, or at several times, to accommodate the crowds. Georgia, the farthest colony, held readings in August.

New York wasn't the only city to rip down visible reminders of the king—across the colonies, people pulled down portraits and tavern signs that showed George III or his coat of arms and smashed and burned them. Georgians held a mock funeral for the king, saying, "[We] commit his political existence to the ground, corruption to corruption, tyranny to the grave, and oppression to eternal infamy; in sure and certain hope that he will never obtain a resurrection to rule again over these United States of America . . ."

The Declaration made a difference. On hearing of independence, New Jersey's Joseph Barton wrote, "Now we know what to depend on. For my part, I have been at a great stand: I could hardly own the King and fight against him at the same time; but now these matters are cleared up. Heart and hand shall move together."

It also had an effect on other nations—for better and for worse. On July 8, Congress sent a copy of the Declaration to Silas Deane of Connecticut, Congress's representative in Paris, telling him to "immediately communicate the piece to the Court of France, and send copies of it to the other Courts of Europe," in hopes of inspiring international support. They also suggested that he get it translated and put in French newspapers. But the letter and copy of the Declaration were lost on the way to France! Congress sent another copy of both on August 7, but they didn't arrive until November 17.

Deane was mortified at the thought of announcing independence to a French court that had known the information for months, thanks to private letters and newspapers. He also thought "two or three Lines from the Committee of Congress in a Letter" wasn't a formal enough way to inform a European court that a new nation had been born. Deane did the best he could, which was to tell the French that Congress had "taken the earliest Opportunity of informing this Court, of the declaration of their Independency," since the original letter had been sent in July. It was an awkward start.

France did not immediately embrace the United States. In fact, the first copies of the Declaration that circulated among the French public were translated anonymously. (There was, after all, that talk of overthrowing kings.) But in a masterful stroke, Congress sent Benjamin Franklin to Paris in the autumn of 1776 to try to negotiate a treaty. A social butterfly, Franklin utterly charmed the French, who gave the Americans a secret loan and began to supply weapons and uniforms. In February 1778, France finally entered a Treaty of Alliance with the United States.

And the British response to the Declaration? The document reached London on August 10, 1776. It was widely printed in British newspapers, sometimes without comment, and sometimes with sarcastic asides. King George III already considered the colonies to be in revolt, and had troops in the field fighting them. That didn't change. In a speech to Parliament on October 26, 1776, he finally addressed the Americans' claim of independence, vowing "to put a speedy End to these Disorders by the most decisive Exertions." He still referred to "my colonies." The English philosopher Jeremy Bentham observed that England ". . . will unite as one man, and teach this rebellious people, that it is one thing for them to *say,* the connection, which bound them to us, is *dissolved,* another to *dissolve* it; that to *accomplish* their *independence* is not quite so easy as to *declare* it. . . ." He was right. It would take George Washington and the Continental Army to make the Declaration stick.

What happened next? The war went badly in late 1776, and Congress waited until the victories at Trenton and Princeton had stabilized the military situation in January 1777 before ordering that authenticated copies should be sent to each state, "with the names of the members . . . subscribing the same" included. They hired Mary Katherine Goddard, a Patriot, to print these official copies. She usually listed herself as "M. K. Goddard" on her newspaper, but the bottom of the Declaration reads "Printed by Mary Katharine Goddard"—the only woman's name on the final text of the Declaration. (Goddard was also the postmistress of Baltimore, making it likely she was the first female US government employee.)

There were more military setbacks in 1777, and in September, British troops entered Philadelphia. Washington's troops spent a hard, frozen winter at Valley Forge, but emerged from camp in 1778 to win two battles near Saratoga, New York. The Continental Army no longer looked like a lost cause, and France now entered the war. Three and a half years later, the British surrendered at Yorktown, Virginia. On September 3, 1783, British and American diplomats signed the Treaty of Paris, ending the war. Britain finally and formally recognized the United States's independence.

IN THE MINDS OF THE PEOPLE

"We hold these truths to be self-evident, that all men are created equal, that they are endowed by their Creator with certain unalienable Rights, that among these are Life, Liberty, and the pursuit of Happiness—That to secure these rights, Governments are instituted among Men." These are enduring American political principles: equality; rights that cannot be taken or given away; the idea that the role of government is to guard the people's rights and help them secure life, liberty, and happiness.

And yet a document that declared all men were created equal was written by a slaveholder and passed by other slaveholders. The Founders continued to wrestle with the contradiction throughout the first years of the nation, even while many of them benefited personally from enslaved people's labor. At the Constitutional Convention in 1787, weeks of debate led to the three-fifths compromise, which counted enslaved people as three-fifths of a person for purposes of congressional representation. Enslaved people couldn't vote, but because representation was based on a state's population, the compromise increased the voting power of slave states. The Constitution also forbade Congress from banning the international slave trade until 1808. Jefferson himself thought slavery's existence threatened the young republic, writing in 1820 that sharp political arguments over the admission of a new slave state filled him with terror, "like a fire bell in the night."

He was right to hear ringing. The generation that fought the Civil War was made up of the grandchildren of the Founders. A Virginia Confederate named George Fitzhugh wrote in 1857, "We do not agree with the authors of the Declaration of Independence, that governments 'derive their just powers from the consent of the governed.' . . . All governments must originate in force, and be continued by force. The very term, government, implies that it is carried on against the consent of the governed." It was an attack on the principles of the Enlightenment, the Declaration, and the Constitution. Union victories in the Civil War, followed by the Thirteenth, Fourteenth, and Fifteenth Amendments, which ended slavery and gave Black Americans citizenship and Black men the right to vote, brought the nation much closer to the ideals stated in the Declaration—especially "all men are created equal."

John Adams wrote to Thomas Jefferson on August 24, 1815, "What do We mean by the Revolution? The War? That was no part of the Revolution. It was only an Effect and Consequence of it. The Revolution was in the Minds of the People, and this was effected, from 1760 to 1775, in the course of fifteen Years before a drop of blood was drawn at Lexington." Adams means that the real revolution wasn't the war itself, but the change in colonists' attitudes. After George Washington was named commander in chief of an army fighting George III's troops, he still routinely toasted the king—until he read *Common Sense*'s indictment of hereditary monarchy. The Declaration followed a spring when towns and colonies demanded independence, one after another. The idea that people could rule themselves, that they had certain inalienable rights—*this* was the revolution. It was a revolution of ideas, a revolution, as Adams said, in the minds of the people.

This American Revolution, and the war that followed it, inspired people around the world, and the Declaration was widely circulated. The first translation was into German and distributed as early as July 6, 1776, for the benefit of Pennsylvania's large German immigrant community. As copies of the Declaration traveled internationally, they reached England first, and from there Scotland, Ireland, and Holland, and then on to German territories, Scandinavia, and Southern and

Eastern Europe. The news hit Warsaw, Poland, within two months. For an age with such slow communication, the Declaration traveled like lightning.

Americans themselves paid little attention to the Declaration as a document in the decades after its passage. The War of 1812, also fought against Great Britain, stimulated a new interest in it, and copies designed for display in government buildings and private homes were printed for the first time. In 1818, John Trumbull's painting of the presentation of the Committee of Five's draft to the Second Continental Congress was exhibited in Boston to large crowds. (It now hangs in the United States Capitol Rotunda.) But once independence was a fact, the Declaration's first and last paragraphs were no longer practically significant, and when wars with Britain ended, the grievances lost their immediacy. President Woodrow Wilson touched on this in 1914: ". . . now nobody anywhere would dare to doubt that we are independent and can maintain our independence. As a declaration of independence, therefore, it is a mere historic document."

But of course, the Declaration was not just an announcement of the birth of a nation; it was also an elegant statement of rights. "We hold these truths to be self-evident . . ." This is the paragraph cited most often as Americans moved into the eras in which slavery ended and women and racial minorities struggled for civil and voting rights. For example, when women's rights advocates gathered in 1848 in Seneca Falls, New York, they wrote a Declaration of Sentiments modeled directly on the Declaration of Independence: "When, in the course of human events, it becomes necessary for one portion of the family of man to assume among the people of the earth a position different from that which they have hitherto occupied, but one to which the laws of nature and of nature's God entitle them . . . We hold these truths to be self-evident; that all men and women are created equal . . ." It also has a lengthy grievance section.

The Declaration of Independence also proved an inspiration to people around the world. Thomas Jefferson was in Paris in 1789, at the beginning of the French Revolution, and worked with the Marquis de Lafayette as he drafted a "Declaration of the Rights of Man and of the Citizen." Lafayette had fought in the American Revolution and was familiar with Jefferson's work; the two documents sound very similar. Lafayette's Declaration served as a statement of ideals and inspiration for the French Revolution, which eventually overthrew King Louis XVI.

And, influenced by both the American and French Revolutions, and in response to their own national histories and issues, people around the world adopted declarations as they threw off colonial oppression. More than a hundred such declarations have been released since 1776. From 1789 to 1848, during what's called "the Age of Revolutions," nations as diverse as Haiti, Greece, and Liberia wrote their own declarations of independence as peoples demanded self-government and democracy and set up republics. When Haiti wrote its declaration in 1804, it became the second independent nation in the Western Hemisphere, after the United States. In Europe, Hungary's startlingly long declaration of 1849 owes a clear debt to Jefferson's work; for example, the first line refers to "inalienable natural rights." It then runs on for more than twenty pages. In contrast, Albania's 1912 declaration of independence from the Ottoman Empire—today known as Turkey—is a single sentence: "Following the speech made by the President, Ismail Kemal Bey, in which he spoke of the great perils facing Albania today, the delegates have all decided unanimously that Albania, as of today, should be on her own, free and independent."

Most declarations made in the twentieth century proclaim a nation's sovereignty, but don't provide a philosophical defense of the rights of individuals. In addressing the rights of both states and people, the US Declaration of Independence has transcended its time. In 1859 Abraham Lincoln wrote, "All honor to Jefferson, to the man who, in the concrete pressure of a struggle for national independence by a single people, had the coolness, forecast, and capacity to introduce into a merely revolutionary document, an abstract truth, applicable to all men and all times."

Adams and Jefferson both died on July 4, 1826—half a century to the day after Congress passed the Declaration. Jefferson had been invited to the fiftieth-anniversary celebration of the Declaration of Independence, held in Washington, D.C. He wasn't well enough to travel, but he sent a letter in which he discusses the Declaration for the last time. He wrote, "*May it be to the world, what I believe it will be . . . the Signal of arousing men to burst the chains under which Monkish ignorance and superstition had persuaded them to bind themselves, and to assume the blessings & security of self-government. . . . All eyes are opened, or opening, to the rights of man. . . . For ourselves, let the annual return of [Independence Day] forever refresh our recollections of these rights and an undiminished devotion to them.*"

What is the legacy of the Declaration of Independence to us today? It's still a clarion call of liberty, the right to overthrow tyrants, the confident statement that the United States of America has no king. Each new generation must renew its commitment to traditional American political principles. Because Adams was right—the revolution was in people's minds and hearts. If we still hold it in ours, a greater nation can yet come forth.

SELECTED WORKS CONSULTED

Allen, Danielle. *Our Declaration: A Reading of the Declaration of Independence in Defense of Equality.* New York: W. W. Norton & Company, 2014.

Armitage, David. *The Declaration of Independence: A Global History.* Cambridge: Harvard University Press, 2007.

Becker, Carl Lotus. *The Declaration of Independence; a Study in the History of Political Ideas.* New York: Alfred A. Knopf, 1969.

Beeman, Richard. *The Penguin Guide to the United States Constitution: A Fully Annotated Declaration of Independence, U.S. Constitution and Amendments, and Selections from The Federalist Papers.* New York: Penguin Books, 2010.

Boyd, Julian P. *The Declaration of Independence: the Evolution of the Text.* Edited by Gerard W. Gawalt. Washington, D.C.: The Library of Congress in association with the Thomas Jefferson Memorial Foundation, Inc., distributed by University Press of New England, 1999.

Ferris, Robert G. *Signers of the Declaration.* Washington, D.C.: United States Department of the Interior, National Park Service, 1973.